WISDOM

from

Fred

"the Lawn Mower Salesman"

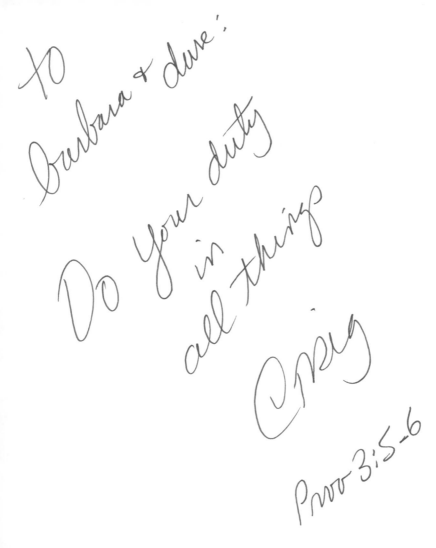

To
Barbara & Dave:

Do your duty
in
all things

Craig

Prov 3:5-6

Craig S. Faubel

WISDOM

from

Fred

"the Lawn Mower Salesman"

Ageless Words to Inspire Success

Wisdom from Fred

"the Lawn Mower Salesman"

Ageless Words to Inspire Success

© 2007 Craig Sterling Faubel
by Craig Sterling Faubel

Manufactured in the United States of America

For information, please contact:
Brown Books Publishing Group
16200 North Dallas Parkway, Suite 170
Dallas, Texas 75248
www.brownbooks.com
972-381-0009
A New Era in Publishing™

ISBN-13: 978-1-933285-76-4
ISBN-10: 1-933285-76-1
LCCN 2006939505
1 2 3 4 5 6 7 8 9 10

For orders, please e-mail Craig at cfaubel6@mac.com
www.craigfaubelintl.com

Every effort has been expended by the compiler to attribute each quote accurately and honestly, but if no attribute is given, it was because the compiler could find no one person known to have coined that quote

Dedication

This book is dedicated to my father-in-law, Col. Benoid E. Glawe Sr. (USMA 1939), to my wife, Maryanne, and our sons, Sterling and Ben, who have been a source of love, encouragement, support, and humor.

Table of Contents

Acknowledgments

To those people who helped to push me out of my comfort zone and who helped to comfort me when I did, thanks to each of you:

To my parents, Jinny and Paul Faubel, who provided a loving environment.

To my brothers, Wil and Steve Faubel, who proved sibling loyalty and honesty.

To my mother-in-law, Mary Glawe, who provided a limitless source of common sense.

To my brothers-in-laws, Michael and Peter Glawe, who provided "older brother" guidance.

To my only aunt and uncle, Mary and John McGrath, who made me speak in front of a mirror to eliminate my stutter.

To my fourth grade teacher, Mrs. Edgar, who made me write "Readers are Leaders" one hundred times.

To my mentor, Bob Kopitke, who had faith in me and gave me the opportunity to be an entrepreneur.

To my advisor, Ed Moerbe, who got me involved in Toastmasters.

To the authors, Brian Tracy, John C. Maxwell, Rick Warren, Jim Collins, Zig Ziglar, and Jim Rohn, who have provided me with a wealth of spiritual, personal, and business growth.

To my protégé, Kristen Laughlin, who was my assistant for almost twenty years and who was a major factor in our business success.

To my "company within a company", Kristen Laughlin, JaNae Adkins, and Jill Bryant—who have been dedicated and loyal to me for nineteen, eleven, and nine years respectively.

To my business associates—Paul Hanning, Jerry Leeds and Paul Cabra.

To my careciple group—Boemers, Elliotts, Evans, Kings, Langfords, Pauls, Riveras, Selaidens and Twists—who provided prayer and fellowship.

To Milli Brown and Kathryn Grant of Brown Book Publishing Group, who encouraged me with my book aspirations.

Preface

In the fourth grade I stubbornly refused to read the book, *Treasure Island*. Because of this my teacher made me write "Readers are Leaders" one hundred times. This proved to be my catalyst in pursuit of books that could help me to grow and to learn. I am an avid reader of the works by Brian Tracy, John C. Maxwell, Jim Rohn, Jim Collins, Zig Ziglar, and Rick Warren. I habitually highlight phrases that make an impact on me and transfer them to my daily journal. I add to that journal any other catch phrases or sayings that I come across. While driving home from a luncheon honoring Bob Buford, the author of *Halftime*, I was reflecting on his message of finding significance in the second half of one's life and I posed the question of significance to myself. "How can I be significant?" I decided to share information that I found significant and important with others. And so *Wisdom from Fred the Lawn Mower Salesman* was born.

The book is divided into ten different categories. Each possesses "golden nuggets of knowledge," which can be applied to life. All of these quotes are the foundation of many successful people and enterprises. The book can be utilized in a variety of ways:

- Promotions at company conventions and meetings

- Common-sense refreshers for business people

- Daily inspirations for salespeople

- Gift books for customers, vendors, and employees

Read one page per day and reflect on, "How can I utilize this quotation in my life?"

My business mission statement is "If you build your people, your people will build your company." I invite you to read and to enjoy this book. Put quotations and sayings into your life.

CRAIG STERLING FAUBEL

P.S. Fred is really Craig. My father-in-law, Col. B.E. Glawe (USMA 1939) thought that my name was Fred and that I sold lawn mowers for a living. My wife and her brothers perpetuated this and left me to fend for myself. The Colonel found out what my name was when he saw the wedding invitation. He unknowingly put life into "Fred."

Faith

Even though I am busy, my relationship with
God deserves top priority above all other demands
on my life.

—Rick Warren—

God has granted to me the serenity to accept the things I cannot change, the courage to change the things I can, and the wisdom to know the difference.

My number one and number two priorities—
God and others.

—Rick Warren—

God's gift to me is my potential.
My gift back to God is what I do with that potential.

I always ask myself
"How will this affect my relationship with God?"

Where faith begins, anxiety ends.

—Rick Warren—

The basis of my goals is spiritual;
based on my relationship and dependence on God.

—Rick Warren—

There are absolutely no conflicts between biblical principles and good business practices.

—Rick Warren—

To whom much is given, much is expected.

—Luke 12:48—

My diligent study of God's Word gives the Holy Spirit an opportunity to direct my steps, develop my character, and deepen my spiritual life.

—John Chrysostom—

Business

The most important single factor in corporate success is faithful adherence to core values. Beliefs must come before goals, policies, and practices.

—Jim Collins—

Integrity is the quality most needed to succeed in life.

The only sacred cow in my business is my basic philosophy of doing business—core ideology.

—Jim Collins—

If I combine a culture of discipline with the ethic of entrepreneurship, I get superior results.

—Jim Collins—

Business goes where it is invited but stays where it is appreciated.

What gets recognized gets repeated.

—Peter Drucker—

Personal growth always precedes
professional growth.

My business grows as I grow personally.

Never let a business decision made by a person whom you hardly know determine how you accept yourself.

I do not let the noise of others' opinions drown out my own inner voice.

—Stephen Jobs—

My personal growth is like investing.
It's not my timing, it's my time in.

1. How I think is everything
2. I decide upon my true dreams and goals
3. I take action
4. I never stop learning
5. I am persistent and work hard

Investor's Business Daily Top Secrets part 1.

6. I learn to analyze details
7. I focus my time and money
8. I am not afraid to innovate
9. I communicate with people effectively
10. I am honest, dependable and take responsibility

Investor's Business Daily Top Secrets part 2

I cannot be a success at work but a failure at home.

Leadership

It's not the size of the company that counts;
it's the size of the leaders within it.

—John C. Maxwell—

Everything rises and falls on leadership.

—John C. Maxwell—

Everyday stressful situations are leadership laboratories.

How I deal with failures determines much of my success as a leader.

Leadership can only function on the basis of trust.

—John C. Maxwell—

Mentoring is good for the team, good for the mentor, and good for the business.

—Scott Snair—

A sign of a well-led company is the consistency and continuity of its leadership.

If I grow the leader, I grow the company.

—John C. Maxwell—

There is no success without a successor.

—Peter Drucker—

As a leader, I need to keep my focus on the customer.

Great leaders always share themselves and what they have learned.

I can always tell my ability to lead others
by how well I lead myself.

If I want to be an effective leader, I must be a servant.

—Rick Warren—

To lead myself, I use my head.
To lead others, I use my heart.

—John C. Maxwell—

Training and managing my mind is the most important skill I will ever have.

—Scott Snair—

Readers are leaders.

—Mrs. Edgar—

I devour books, biographies, success books, and sales books.

How do I become more valuable?
By investing in myself.

For me to earn more, I must learn more.

—Brian Tracy—

If I build myself consistently,
my business will grow exponentially.

—Mike Litman—

Employees

I will not become rich unless I enrich another.

I fill a business office with life, energy, and enthusiasm—not ego.

The growth and development of my people
is the highest calling of my leadership.

Company success = employees first, customers second, and stockholders third.

—Jim Collins—

My most important task as a leader is to acquire, develop, and keep good people.

—John C. Maxwell—

No executive has ever suffered because his subordi-
nates were strong and effective.

—Peter Drucker—

If I produce other leaders, my influence is multiplied.

How can I make you more productive, profitable,
and give you a competitive advantage?

—Mark Cuban—

The fruit of my work grows on other people's trees.

My greatest achievements are those that benefit others.

I must maintain unwavering faith that I can and will prevail in the end, regardless of the difficulty, and at the same time have the discipline to confront the most brutal facts of my current reality.

—Jim Collins—
The Stockdale Paradox

My most important customers are my employees.
If I take care of my employees, my employees will
take care of my customers.

—Herb Kelleher—

I have never seen a company that was able to satisfy its customers that did not also satisfy its employees.

My employees will treat my customers no better than I treat my employees.

The people who know the business best
are the people who are closest to the business.

—Brad Smith—

Preparation prevents pressure,
procrastination produces it.

—Rick Warren—

I hire the attitude and teach the business.

I don't look for "yes men."
I want team members to share concerns, voice objections, and make recommendations.

In determining the "right people,"
I give greater weight to character attributes than
educational background or work experience.

Progress and innovation are made by people who think beyond their boundaries.

If I put fences around my good people,
I will get sheep.

I give my people the room they need, and I encourage individual initiative.

Progress comes from people who think
against the grain.

—Saw Ken Wye—

I always assign a task that will stretch
a person's ability.

There is no future in any job, the future lies in the man who holds the job.

—George Crane—

If I build my people, my people will build my company.

—Craig Faubel—

Referrals and repeats will make you rich.

—Craig Faubel—

I treat every person I meet as if he or she were the most important person in the world.

Relationships are what life is all about.

—Jerry Manas—

Few things will pay bigger dividends than the time
and trouble I take to understand people.

My friends are precious.

—Randy Twist—

Every person I meet has the potential
to teach me something.

My success will ultimately depend on the relationships I build with people.

I listen for both content and feeling,
not only what is being said.

I listen for the message
and the message behind the message.

Ideas are a dime a dozen but the people who implement them are priceless.

—Josh Ridker—

I do my best work just by listening.

My listening to others builds trust and relationships.

I must listen twice as much as I speak.

Remember that a person's name is to that
person the sweetest and most important sound
in any language.

—Dale Carnegie—

Customers

If I focus on whatever it is to satisfy the customer,
I will have the competitive edge.

My customers want a relationship with me first.

—Brian Tracy—

I treat my customers like my best friends.

I always exceed customer expectations.

I cannot put a dollar value on keeping
my clients happy.

—Mark Cuban—

My client's don't care how much I know until they know how much I care.

—John C. Maxwell—

Inspirational/ Attitude

If it's to be, it's up to me.

—Michael Angier—

The only one who is stopping me is me.

My attitude is everything.

All significant battles are waged within me first.

—John C. Maxwell—

How big I think determines the size
of my accomplishments.

—John C. Maxwell—

It's my attitude, not my aptitude,
that will determine my altitude.

—Zig Ziglar—

My attitude determines the atmosphere;
my values determine my decisions.

I realize that the only thing I have is absolute control over my attitude.

My success depends on many things,
but mostly it depends on me.

The true measure of me is not how long my candle burns but how brightly it burns.

What lies behind me in the past and what lies before me in the future are small matters compared to what lies within me.

—Brian Tracy—

The value of my life is not in the length of days but in the use I make of them.

I do not know what the future holds,
but I know who holds the future.

—Rick Warren—

The size of the problem is never the issue.
What matters is the size of me.

—John C. Maxwell—

I hold the belief that I must act right whatever the consequences.

—Robert E. Lee—

The last of one's freedom is to choose one's attitude in any given circumstance.

—Victor Frankl—

Goals

My happiness, wealth, and success
are my by-products of goal setting.

—John C. Maxwell—

I set my goals in concrete, but I write my plans in sand.

I am always planning, always looking ahead, but always allow for the possibility of midcourse corrections.

When I write down my goals and actions, my conscious and subconscious minds are then engaged.

—Brian Tracy—

My conscious goals need to be my subconscious goals.

The reason I set goals is for what they will make of me once I achieve them.

Will this activity help me achieve one of my goals?

—Brent Drees—

I have four goals of life: to live, to love, to learn,
and to leave a legacy.

—Stephen Covey—

It is what I focus on that expands.

—Brian Tracy—

The art of being wise is knowing what to overlook.

—William James—

Growth

The definition of insanity—continuing to do the same thing and expecting things to be different.

—Rapport Leadership Intl.—

If I always do what I have done,
I always get what I have always got.

I don't win today's ballgame with yesterday's base hits.

Who I am and what I do today determines
where I will be tomorrow.

I can reach potential tomorrow if I dedicate myself to growth today.

I don't go through life, I grow through life.

I am either green and growing or ripe and rotting.

—Ray Kroc—

I am always learning, always improving,
always open to change.

Change is a given; growth is a choice.

In order for me to grow as a person,
I must expand my comfort zone.

I cannot explore my potential and expand it without taking a risk.

I eliminate my fear of getting out of my comfort zone.

I only go on expeditions that make me grow.

My problems always create my opportunities to learn, to grow, and to improve.

—John C. Maxwell—

The price of progress for me is the pain of change.

The ultimate measure of me is not where I stand in the moments of comfort and convenience, but where I stand at times of challenge and controversy.

—Rev. Martin Luther King—

It's the management of fear, not the absence of fear, that helps me get through life.

My life is a series of tests.

It's not so much what happens in my life that matters; it is how I respond to what happens.

The quality of my life is determined by how I respond to changes and tough situations.

It is important to learn from my mistakes; it is even more important to learn from the mistakes of others.

My test is not in the attack but in my response.

My life is a test, a trust, a temporary residence.

—Rick Warren—

My only way out is through.

The price of success is less than the price of failure.

—Zig Zigler—

Failure is not an option for me.

—The *Odyssey* movie—

The pain of my discipline weighs ounces,
but the pain of my regret weighs tons.

—Jim Rohn—

The secret of my success is found in my daily agenda.

If I fail to plan, I plan to fail.

—Reverend Steve Mathewson—

Time management is really personal management,
life management, and management of myself.

—Brian Tracy—

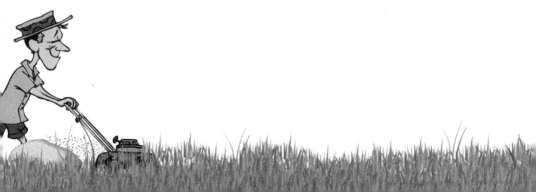

I always . . .

I always stand up for what is right.

Whatever it is, I always do the right thing,
no matter the cost.

I always surround myself with the best people
I can find.

I always try to be friends with everybody.

I always have to pay a price for growth.

I always get what I pay for.

I always put in four hours of preparation
for one hour of presentation.

I always do the most good that I can where I am.

I always travel on the road less traveled.

I always have a choice.

I must always (1) do what is right, (2) do the best I can, and (3) treat others the way I want to be treated.

—Lou Holtz—

I always seek the seed of triumph in every adversity.

—Brian Tracy—

I seek to change, to grow, to learn, and to love.

—Rick Warren—

I seek responsibility and take responsibility for my actions.

The three questions I ask of myself:
(1) Who am I?
(2) Where am I going?
(3) Why am I going there?

—Kevin Cashman—

I never burn my bridges.

I never give up. I never, never give up.
I never, never, never give up.

—Winston Churchill—

I will not lie, cheat, steal, or tolerate anyone
who does.

—United States Military Academy—

I will invest more in myself than I do in my career.

I will act now. I will act now. I will act now =
No Opportunity Wasted.

—Stephen Pierce—

I am my values expressed in action.

I don't want to become a person of success;
I want to become a person of value.

—Mike Litman—

In order for me to live a worthwhile, meaningful life, I must be a part of something greater than myself.

If I can dream it, I can do it.

—Quentin Eyers—

I want to be impressed and interested,
not impressive and interesting.

I will be a "meaningful specific"
rather than a "wandering generality."

—Brian Tracy—

I either affect people or infect people.

Instead of putting difficult people in their place,
I put myself in their place.

I can get everything in life that I want if I can help others get what they want.

—Zig Ziglar—

I accept complete responsibility for myself and for everything that happens to me.

—Brian Tracy—

If I don't make my own decisions in life, somebody else will make them for me.

I make a living by what I get. I make a life
by what I give.

—President George W. Bush—

I become what I think about most of the time—
if I change my thinking, I change my life.

—Brian Tracy—

My thoughts determine my feelings, my feelings determine my actions, my actions determine my results, and my results determine my destiny.

—T. Harv Eker—

I choose my thoughts.

No thought lives in my mind rent free.

I think first, speak last.

I write it down. I write it down. I write it down.

Do I have the ability to choose the
"harder right" rather than the "easy wrong"?

—United States Military Academy—

My integrity is the quality most needed for me to succeed in business.

If I take care of my character,
my reputation will take care of itself.

—John C. Maxwell—

I am always judged by the company I keep.

General

There are no traffic jams on the extra mile.

—Zig Ziglar—

The other person's perception is reality.

—Jeffrey Gitomer—

Givers gain; takers lose.

—Rapport Leadership Intl.—

To reach the juiciest apples, I have to climb high, reach out, and risk falling off the ladder.

Together
Everyone
Accomplishes
More

—Mike Ditka—

It's not what I know; it's who knows me.

See the future
Engage and develop people
Reinvent continuously
Value results and relationships
Embody values

—Ken Blanchard and Mark Miller—

Individuals win trophies; teamwork wins pennants.

Great people talk about ideas; average people talk about themselves; small people talk about others.

—Arthur Friedman—

The heart of the matter is the matter of the heart.

Men of genius are admired.
Men of wealth are envied.
Men of power are focused.
But only men of character are trusted.

—Mike Litman—

Nothing happens until something is sold.

—Bryan Flanagan—

What is the best use of my time right now?

—Brian Tracy—

My outer world tends to be a mirror image
of my inner world.

—Brian Tracy—

Who I am is more important than what I do.

I survived the torture and brutality in the concentration camps because of three things:
I never gave up hope, I never gave up my belief, and I was always positive.

—Mendel Jakubowicz—
Holocaust survivor

My life is a marathon, not a sprint.

—Rick Warren—

The quality of my life is determined by
the depth of my commitment to excellence,
no matter what my chosen field.

—Vince Lombardi—

School is never out.

—Jinny & Paul Faubel—
My Mom & Dad

Without my health,
all the riches in the world are worth nothing.

Success equals uncommon application
of common knowledge.

FEAR= False Evidence Appearing Real.

—Rapport Leadership Intl.—